The Social Media HandBook

Harness the power of Social media to grow your small business

FRANK DAPPAH

The Social Media Handbook

Copyright © 2019 Ostrich Publishers

All rights reserved.

ISBN: 9781089492573

Ostrich Publishers
Made in the U.S.A
www.ostrichpress.com

READ THIS BOOK IF...

- You wish to learn how to use Social media to acquire more customers for your small business

- You want to know how other companies like yours have used the power of Social Media to grow their bottom lines

- You want to find out more about the opportunities social media has to offer.

- You want to learn how to set up effective Social Media campaigns

- You are ready to grow your business, period.

The Social Media Handbook

The
Social Media HandBook

Harness the power of Social media to grow your small business

FRANK DAPPAH

DEDICATIONS

This book is dedicated to Regina & Ebenezer Cudjoe. Thanks for being the source of my confidence and the inspiration that drives my ambition even till today.

Thanks!

CONTENTS

PREFACE	I DON'T LIKE CHANGE	6
CHAPTER 1	THE HISTORY OF SOCIAL MEDIA	12
CHAPTER 2	HERE AND NOW	24
CHAPTER 3	THE POWER OF SOCIAL MEDIA	31
CHAPTER 4	SOCIAL IS UNIQUE	48
CHAPTER 5	INSTAGRAM: BUILD YOUR INSTAGRAM FOLLOWING	67
CHAPTER 6	ANATOMY OF AN EFFECTIVE SOCIAL MEDIA AD + EXAMPLES	75
CHAPTER 7	THESE GUYS GET IT: COMPANIES THAT HAVE USED SOCIAL MEDIA EFFECTIVELY	93
CHAPTER 8	GET MORE VIEWS ON YOUTUBE	105
CHAPTER 9	USE LINKEDIN NATIVE VIDEO TO REACH NEW AUDIENCES	112
CHAPTER 10	HASHTAG YOUR WAY TO SUCCESS	127
CHAPTER 11	SETTING OBJECTIVES AND MEASURING SUCCESS	136
TAHNK YOU		141

The Social Media Handbook

PREFACE

I DON'T LIKE CHANGE

I am not completely certain when or how this happened. I don't know, I guess the uncertainty of it all scares the crap out of me and annoys me at the same time.

As I get older, it seems change is an endeavor of which I wish more and more to have no part.

The problem is, born in the '80s, I am still relatively young, but old enough to remember a time when we all spoke to each other face-to-face. A time when children went outside to play.

We told each other in (words) when we liked something and not with a click of the mouse. A time when "getting poked" had a whole different meaning. Forgive me if I sound like a Luddite.

I know what you are thinking; "How is this guy

going to teach me anything about technology or Social media? He seems to be as uncomfortable with technology as I am". I start this book this way, as my way of letting you know, that I feel your pain.

That is if your pain involves wondering if the confusion and newness of this whole "social media thing" is worth the trouble?

I understand your trepidation.

I am here, however, to let you know that the opportunity that social media has to offer is far too great to ignore. There are literally billions of people out there just waiting to hear what you have to say. No lie! Social media has become the means by which we all communicate these days. So be the man or woman in the arena! Jump in, learn how to use social media to grow your business and you will be glad you did.

WE ARE ALL GATHERED HERE

In this day and age, I don't think any serious small business owner, or entrepreneur can afford not to have a sound, even aggressive social media marketing strategy.

I am serious. Far too many people all around the world spend so much time on apps like Facebook, Twitter, and Instagram for you to miss out on the opportunity to present your services to them.

According to the social media consultancy firm, Hootsuite, an estimated 3.5 billion people use social media each year. That's about 45% of the overall population of the world. Picture that. Almost half of the population of the world is on social media. They access these platforms in order to keep up with current events and to connect with friends and family.

About 61 percent of that total number of social media users access various social platforms via mobile devices.

The countries with the most active social media users compared to the total population are **South Korea, U.A.E, Taiwan, Hong Kong, and Singapore.**

    I bring this up now to help introduce an idea that I like to share with most entrepreneurs I meet: Go global! There is so much opportunity out there outside the borders of your home country.

    Now, I will admit, some businesses are not well-suited to having a global customer base, but I think there is tremendous potential value in carefully considering if you can somehow position your business to meet the needs of a global audience.

    If you operate a brick-and-mortar business like a restaurant, perhaps there is some way to partner with vendors in other countries to have some of your signature sauces and dishes made and shipped to folks in that country. This is just an idea of course. The point is, you need to think about going global. There is a whole new world out there, and the power of social media will help you reach that elusive global marketplace.

A KICK IN THE PANTS

To say that profitability is essential to the survival of your business would be stating the obvious.
But would I though? I mean, as entrepreneurs, small business owners, go-getters, etc. Regardless of your preferred moniker, do you really realize and appreciate this reality? Your business needs to make money, period.

That being said, every profitability origin story starts with growth. Affordable, manageable growth. That's the way to do it. So now that we are all on the same page about the importance of growth and subsequently, profitability, how do we get there?

For some, profitability might be a continuous quest for improvement. For others, running a profitable business might be a destination they seek to reach for the first time, some day in the future. No matter which of these two situations you currently find yourself in, I think we can all agree that your business needs to bring in more money this year than it did last year. Enough to cover your cost of doing business, plus pay yourself and your employees, if you have any.

For this reason, every business, no matter how profitable needs to keep bringing in more customers and selling more stuff to those customers. For businesses around the world, there are many ways (all working at once) to give their businesses the proverbial, perpetual kick in the pants it needs.

Larger corporations will hire large teams to go out and constantly try to find ways to grow the bottom line.

For years, true growth via marketing has been a privilege reserved only for a chosen, deep-pocketed few. The explosion of the internet around the world and the ubiquity of social media and mobile devices has changed all that.

Now, even small businesses like yours can also get their products and services in front of folks across the globe for pennies on the dollar.

In this book, I will cover three main topics.
I will share with you some information about the size, trends, and future of social media. I will also show you how to set up effective social media campaigns and help you understand what makes a successful social media ad. I will also help put you on the path to building your very own social media campaigns.

The Social Media Handbook

CHAPTER ONE

THE HISTORY OF SOCIAL MEDIA

THE EARLY DAYS

Social media, in one form or another, has been with us since the early days of the internet itself. Creating connections between humans and the sharing of ideas and information has always been the founding purpose of the world wide web.

We built this great technology for the sole purpose of connecting and relating to one another. From the days of CompuServe till now, this is what we spend most of our online time doing. connecting to other humans. The need to communicate and form tribes is as natural to us as a species as breathing. Let's face it, we are pack animals. The early days of the Internet saw many inventions all aimed at satisfying our need to connect.

BULLETIN BOARDS, FORUMS, AND CHATROOMS

Bulletin Board Systems or BBSes can be considered as the very first iteration of Social media. These were essential pieces of software that users could download to their computers. They could then post messages to a central system for other users to see and respond to. Phone lines were used as a means for connection in the early days of the Internet. Back when "Long distance calling" was a thing that cost you a little extra on your phone bill.

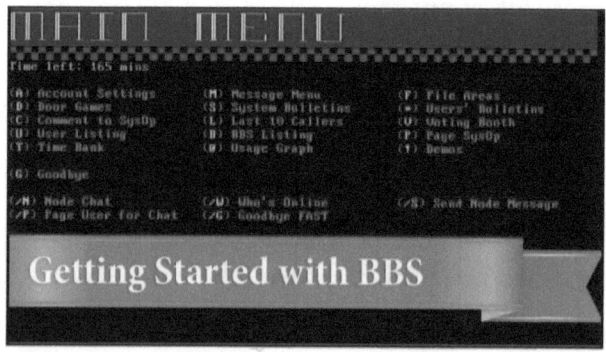

BBS (Bulletin board system)

If you are under the age of 25 reading this book, let me stop to assure you that you read that last statement correctly. Calling outside your area code was considered "Long distance" and thus required a special carrier who charged extra. As a result, most BBS systems were localized. These Bulletin board systems became very popular in the '80s and '90s. Services like ***Tom Jennings' FidoNet*** become dominant players in the space.

FidoNet was a worldwide computer network that was used to communicate between BBS systems. The system essentially linked many Bulletin board systems together, thus allowing folks from various different BBSes to connect. Other notable acts like **CompuServe** also became essential elements on the quest to allow more interconnectivity among humans on the world wide web.

FidoNet BBS mainframe

CompuServe was launched in 1969 as Compu-Serv Network, Inc. in Columbus, Ohio, as a subsidiary of Golden United Life Insurance.

Although there is some debate as to who can be credited with the creation of CompuServe, many identify Golden United founder **Harry Gard, Sr.** As the father of the computer network system. CompuServe was started as a business-only mainframe in the '70s but became available to the general public in the late '80s.

CompuServe Ads and posters

CompuServe, via an earlier version of Email, provided a means by which users could send messages back and forth to one another. The service also provided users with other platforms on which to express themselves such as chatrooms and online forums.

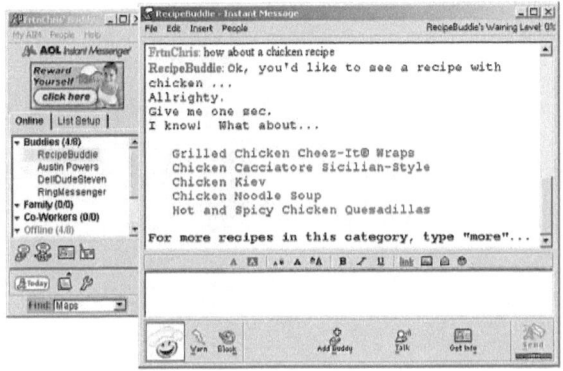

AOL Instant Massager Applet

The '90s would usher in the very first version of true social media: AOL (America Online). AOL provided a whole host of Social media-like services like AOL Instant messenger, Forums with complete user profiles, chatrooms, and many more.

AOL was extremely popular among younger audiences. The use of Emoticons (Emojis) to express oneself also become poplar. I remember, I would get right on the AOL chatrooms after school, back then. I was in High School then.

Yahoo would also, during the same era follow in AOL's footsteps and launch their own Instant messenger app.

Along with many of the same features that were widely liked during those days. There were Yahoo User groups, forums, and message boards.

THE BIRTH OF TRUE SOCIAL MEDIA

I believe that most industry observers and experts will agree with me when I say that the first truly social media site was **Classmates.com**. A first of its kind web portal that provided the tools needed for one to reconnect with their old classmates.

The site, however, in the beginning, did not allow users to create detailed personal profiles. The idea took off almost immediately. The site is still active even today with over 5 million active users.

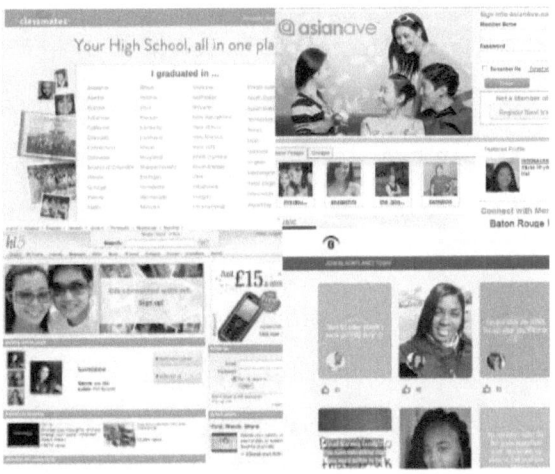

The success of Classmates.com would cause

other players to get into the game as well. Although, newer social networking sites at the time focused on specific niches. Sites like **Asianave.com**, founded in 1997 promised to connect Asian Americans.

Then came youth-focused sites like **HI5** and **Blackplanet.com** around 1999, and **Migente.com** in 2000. Blackplanet still has over 8 million users.

SOCIAL MEDIA IS HERE TO STAY

Different folks have their own opinions on how the "Social Media" we have come to know and love today, for better or for worse, actually evolved. Absolute historical accuracy is not what I am going for here.

My goal is to simply provide you with some historical context based on my research. I also want to let you know that social media has been with us for a while now, and it is here to stay.

Why am I doing this? Why am I taking you down memory lane? I want you to not look at Social media as a thing for young people, a passing fad, but rather as a well-established means for you to connect with new customers. Sort of the way you think of T.V or radio.

CHAPTER TWO

HERE AND NOW

CIRCLE OF FRIENDS

In 2002, Jonathan Abrams launched **Friendster.com**. The first of its kind social media platform. Friendster was very different from anything the world had seen before. For one, the site allowed users to create full-blown, detailed personal profiles.

The site was also organized around the " Circle of friends" principle. The idea was that true social connections could only be made between folks with common bonds. Common interests, common friends, etc. An Idea that still remains the prevalent organizing principle on which most current social media apps are built.

In its heyday, Friendster amassed an enviable 5 million plus active users and has since undergone a slew of cosmetic, as well as fundamental changes. The site is still active even today, but now serves as an online gaming destination.

LinkedIn was launched in 2003 to be a

meeting place for business folk and professionals. The main difference between LinkedIn and other social media sites, even from the beginning is the site's more serious, professional tone.

LinkedIn brings folks together and provides tools for them to connect with other professionals, find employment or business opportunities, and to promote their businesses. The platform was recently purchased by Microsoft. LinkedIn now has over 500 million members with 260 million LinkedIn users logging in each month.

Myspace was also introduced to the public on August 1st, 2003, by Tom Anderson, Chris DeWolfe, and Jon Hart. Myspace had a significant influence on pop culture and music and created a computer game platform that launched the successes of Zynga and RockYou, among others. At onetime the clear leader in the social media space, the site focused on attracting young adults and music lovers.

The site was one of the first social media

platforms to provide users with ways and means to create and share rich media like GIF's and videos. Over the years, Myspace fell out of favor with most young people at that time flocking to the newly launched, much cooler Facebook. Even today, Myspace still has over 50 million active users.

Facebook was launched out of a Harvard dorm room on February 4, 2004. Created by fellow Harvard College students and roommates; Mark Zuckerberg, Eduardo Saverin, Andrew McCollum, Dustin Moskovitz, and Chris Hughes, the site initially sought to connect college students and required one to have a college email address to join. Some observers believe that the earlier aura of exclusivity helped make the site more popular among its core demographic of young adults.

In 2006, membership to Facebook was opened to anyone over the age of 13 with an email address. The name of the site was derived from the face book directories often given to American university students. The social media platform with its simplistic design and easy-to-use interface instantly became a crowd favorite and caught the eye and checkbook of the early investor and PayPal Co-founder, Peter Thiel.

In 2012, Facebook went public at a valuation of over $100 billion, the largest valuation to date for a newly listed public company. The success of Facebook ushered in a new era in social media, helping launch the likes of Twitter, Instagram, Snapchat, and many more.

WHAT TO EXPECT GOING FORWARD

In the following chapters of this book, I will attempt to provide you with a wealth of information, tips and guides to help you win at social media marketing.

I will provide you with a practical guide to help you setup and launch, both free and paid marketing campaigns. I will provide you with information on some strategies that have worked for me in the past, and ones I currently use. Although most of the information I share can be used with most social media platforms, I will focus on the top three or five that I use frequently. Here, I am talking about **Facebook, Twitter, Instagram, LinkedIn, and Pinterest**. I will do so to make things simpler for both of us. You will notice that in some lists, I will leave out some platforms that will make you think; "Hey, what about XYZ platform?" Don't worry if at any given time I do not specifically talk about any one platform. Assume the data I am providing includes that one app you were thinking about. My ultimate goal is for you to have a general strategic overview of the power of the top platform out there and a path forward for you to approach your social media marketing plans.

CHAPTER THREE

THE POWER OF SOCIAL MEDIA

IT'S A DIGITAL WORLD OUT THERE

In this book, and in a few chapters, I talk a lot about "harnessing the power of social media". We entrepreneurs often speak of the opportunities to grow our companies, opportunities available via the power of social media, and the enormous amounts of worldwide subscribers most of these platforms hold. This leads to the question: How powerful is Social media?

The truth is, social media holds more sway over our daily lives than most people realize. We come to a whole host of important decisions on a daily basis based on content shared by our friends and family, or by the organizations that choose to communicate with us via social media. Today, most of us from our opinions about Politicians, celebrities, products, and brands based on the prevailing consensus on our favorite social media platforms.

Even our News media outlets, these days seem to take their direction as to which topics to cover based on the trending topics of the day. Careful and deliberate news analysis has been replaced by Hashtags and Likes. Outlets like Huffington post and Elite Daily seem to make the decision to cover topics simply because they are being talked about on Twitter or Facebook. That being said, since these platforms are the venue for most of the conversations taking place around the world, why not take this opportunity to capitalize on the ubiquity of social media.

I AM GETTING TOO OLD FOR THIS

I can understand why most of the small business owners and entrepreneurs I meet find the whole "Social media marketing" thing to be so freaking confusing. I mean, Gosh, there seem to be about a thousand platforms out there, and if you are getting up there in age like I am, you easily get overwhelmed by the sheer multitude of available options when it

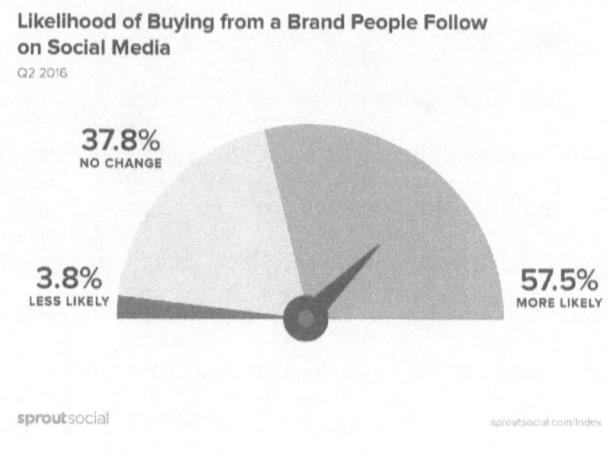

comes to social media apps.

What I have, over time, realized though is that there really are only about five or so platforms worth exploring as a means to advertise. Sure, there are many cool social media applications on the market but only a few that will give you the tools you need to promote your business, products, and services.

In this chapter, we shall take a closer look at the social media platforms that I consider to be business friendly.

#NOTMYCUSTOMERS?

Though it may seem as if social media is purely a young-people thing, studies actually show that social media attracts consumers of all ages and backgrounds. Sure, in the past, apps like Twitter, Facebook, and Instagram have been the playgrounds of teenagers and twenty-somethings, over time things have changed quite a bit. Today, many different kinds of people of all income levels and ethnicities use social media as a means to communicate.

Business leaders use social media to put out press releases and other official statements, celebrities communicate with their fans via social media, even a certain president insists on only communicating via Twitter. Regardless of who your target audience is, or who your potential customers might be, chances are, they are on social media.

Consider this:

Twitter

- According to Pew Internet Research, 29% of internet users with college degrees use Twitter.

- In the United States, slightly more women than men use Twitter.

- In Great Britain, 59% of Twitter users are men, while 41% are women.

- Internationally, the trend follows Great Britain. 57% of global Twitter users are men, while 42% are women.

- 52% of women in their twenties in Japan use Twitter, but that number drops sharply to 36% after age 30.

- 53% of male Twitter users use the platform to receive news, compared to 47% of female Twitter users.

- 40% of U.S. adults who use Twitter are aged

between 18 and 29 years. That's more than any other age group.

- Usage among U.S. adults drops as age increases. Pew research found that 27% of those aged 30-49, 15% of those aged 50-64, and 8% of those aged 65 and above use Twitter (down from 10% in 2016).

- In Great Britain, Twitter users are young. The majority of Twitter users in Great Britain are under 34 years of age.

- 43% of 30-49-year-olds Twitter users use the platform to receive news.

- 32% of U.S. teens use Twitter, but only 3% say it's the platform they use most often.

YouTube

- YouTube reaches more 18- to 34-year-olds than any cable network in the U.S.

- 1.9 billion logged-in users visit YouTube every month

That's half the internet. And every day, they watch a billion hours of video.

- 96 percent of 18- to 24-year-old American internet users use YouTube

Essentially every Gen Z'er with an internet connection is on the platform. *This is not so surprising, given that historically YouTube has been very, very free.*

Meanwhile, traditional TV is still on the decline: weekly watch time dropped 12 percent among 18- to 34-year-olds in 2018; and in 2017 it dropped 13 percent.

- YouTube is the 2nd most-visited website in existence, according to Alexa

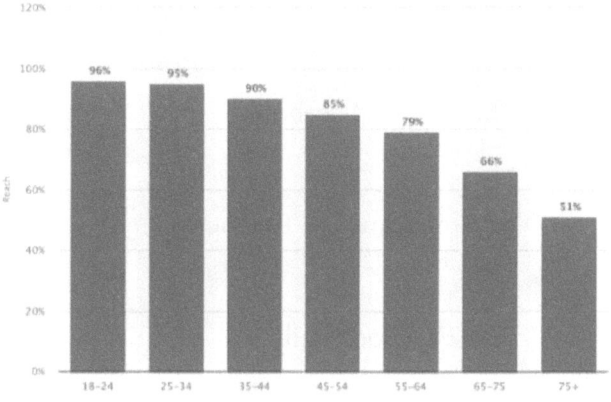

For your reference, this is the percentage of every American age demographic using YouTube, as of January 2018:

Facebook

- 13% of global active Facebook users are women ages 25–34

- India has the highest number of Facebook

users in the world

- 51% of teens use Facebook

- 68% of Americans use Facebook

- 74% visit Facebook daily

See more Facebook user demographics at:

https://sproutsocial.com/insights/facebook-stats-for-marketers/

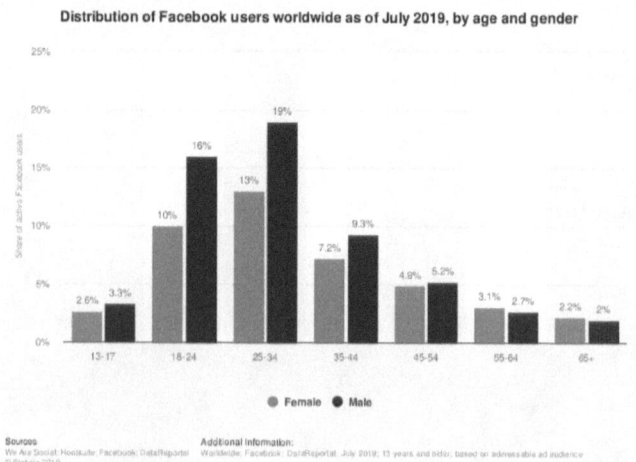

Instagram

- 1 billion people use Instagram every month

- 88% of users are outside the U.S.

-

- 71% of Instagram users around the globe are under the age of 35

- 72% of U.S. teens use Instagram

- 95% of U.S. Instagrammers use YouTube

- 35% of online adults use Instagram

See more Instagram user demographics at:
https://blog.hootsuite.com/instagram-statistics/

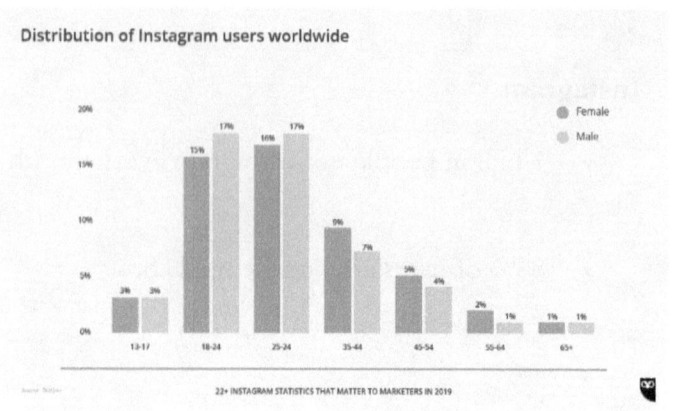

OPEN FOR BUSINESS

Here is a realization one comes to only after spending thousands of dollars and countless hours checking out most of the social media tools out there. One can only find this out by engaging in some good old-fashioned trial and error, so let me save you some time and money by sharing some valuable information with you.

Before you start to even think about setting up your social media campaigns, I ask that you make a shortlist of the platforms that are most conducive to small business activities.

So, what does it mean for a social media platform to be business-friendly? Simple, these are the social media companies that have taken the time to create tools specifically aimed at helping small businesses reach their target audiences.

Facebook is the obvious leader in this area. However, there are others that not only provide the tools and features needed to promote your business, but they also help reach niche groups. LinkedIn, for instance, is great for promoting business-to-business products and services. This is due to the fact that the platform's members are mostly serious professionals, Leaders of industry, small business owners and entrepreneurs.

Social media platforms built to help promote small business

Facebook

Facebook, in my book is the most business-friendly social media platform out there. Over the last ten years or so, the company has been hard at work building tools to help small businesses attract new customers and engage with current ones.

Their well-known "business pages" tool is great for any small business to launch an array of affordable marketing campaigns. And since Facebook determines the cost to market based on location, among other factors, it can be quite cheap to find new customers overseas.

The company also has various marketing programs to help promote your business locally.

Pinterest

Pinterest is great for businesses that sell highly visual products. So, here we are talking about art, fashion, architectural services, travel, and hospitality products, etc.

A popular hub for creatives, the platform allows businesses to easily set up shareable advertising campaigns. Businesses of all types can also set up Professional pages to help grow their following.

Instagram

Instagram is another "Visual" social media platform. The app is popular among younger audiences. Instagram is also quite popular around the world, with most of its users logging on from outside the United States. Their "Instagram for business" platform provides marketers and small business owners with many options to create and deploy robust marketing campaigns. Business users can create Stories Ads, Photo Ads, Video Ads, Carousel Ads, and Collection Ads. All of Instagram's ad programs allow you to target people based on specific locations like states, provinces, cities or countries.

You can also reach people based on interests like apps they use, ads they click and accounts they follow. And if you have an existing customer list, you can run ads to your customers based on their email addresses or phone numbers.

Twitter

Twitter is probably my second favorite social media platform to advertise on. The first being Facebook of course. Twitter is great for targeting what I call " Vocal audiences", the type of prospective customer who knows what they want and wants what they know. The platform is great for folks who love to read and delve deeper into their favorite topics.

The Twitter Ads interface provides businesses with the tools needed to build dedicated business pages as well as the ability to directly advertise to your desired audience. For one, you can use targeting features to choose the audience you want to reach. Select geographic areas, the followers of a notable account, or target people's interests. Twitter Ads run in an auction.

Decide how much you will pay for each interaction, such as a new follower or a click to your website. Or use automatic bidding, which determines the best bid cost based on your budget and goals. Select the Tweets you want to focus on in your campaign. Choosing 4 to 5 is a good start. Include strong call-to-actions, like "sign up" or "start today." Avoid #hashtags or @mentions in your copy so that your audience does not click away from your ad.

CHAPTER FOUR

SOCIAL IS UNIQUE

SOCIAL IS A LITTLE DIFFERENT

There are many folks out there who have either given up on the whole " Social media" marketing thing or are just about ready to. I mean, this stuff doesn't work, right? And who can blame you for feeling this way? Everywhere you look, you see folks who seem to be making money, getting people to buy their products and services with just a few tweets or Facebook posts.

You tried it. You told your friends via Facebook

post about your upcoming fashion show and they don't seem to care. In fact, no one seems to give a damn about any of your business ventures, you know, the ones you can't seem to stop tweeting about. After a while you get tired of pretending to make things happen and quit. This is quite a common phenomenon among many entrepreneurs.

In this chapter, I will try to answer the question of what you are doing wrong and share some strategies on how to make all those posts work for you.

AS SEEN ON TV

I love ads. Don't judge me. I analyze all kinds of advertising. I study online ads as well as Television and radio commercials. I like breaking them down to see what makes the effective ones, well, effective, and what causes others to fail to have the intended impact. Though to the untrained eye, all ads may look, sound, and smell the same - Yes, smell. Ever been to the Mall around Christmas time? Something in the air just puts you in the mood to shop, right?

That's that " Forget your credit card bills and shop" by Calvin Klein. Anyway, where was I? Oh yes, there are major differences on how ads are created. On whom the intended audience of the ad is, and the medium the ad will be rolled out on.

There are two main kinds of advertising: The first ones provide information for you to buy something that you are already looking for, think Google Ads, and if you are old enough, telephone directories. Then, there are ads that seek to interrupt whatever you were doing to tell you about this new, awesome deal. Television, radio, and social media ads fall into this second category.

These ads are therefore aimed at a target audience based on certain demographics and psychographic factors and are built to provide you with an offer you can't refuse. Advertisers will promise you a risk-free, and quick experience. I will go into detail in the next chapters about how you will need to craft your social media ads, for this type of ad, to get the results you want, but for now, know the main difference between all other online ads and social media ads.

PAID MARKETING IS YOUR FRIEND

A big mistake I often see entrepreneurs make, there is this strange prevailing theory among some that goes like this. Some seem to have this belief that they can build a huge profitable business just off free marketing. I strongly disagree with this position. I mean, yeah, you can get the word out about your products and services through free promotions, word-of-mouth, and well-placed press releases. A 2016 survey of 168 Chief Marketing Officers revealed that marketing budgets account for as much as 40 percent of a firm's budget, with a median of 10 percent of the overall budget and a mean average of 12 percent. To be able to acquire new customers at a significant, easy to track pace, one must have a sound paid advertising strategy.

In other words; Pay for marketing in addition to your current promotional activities. It doesn't hurt to do both.

Social media marketing is no different. It is not enough to simply share information about your products with your friends and/or fans. You need to carve out a budget, however little it may be, to pay for marketing.

The great thing about Social is that depending on your target audience and their geographical location, it can pretty inexpensive to create effective marketing campaigns to reach them. Facebook, Instagram, and Twitter have great marketing programs to do just that.

Below, I will outline some of the individual marketing programs available on these three social media platforms.

Facebook

Facebook is probably the most robust Social media platform out there in terms of the advertising options marketers can access on the platform. Over the last decade, or so, the company has really built out all marketing avenues. With the acquisition of Instagram as well as the introduction of Facebook Stories, small businesses now have several options to reach new audiences both local and global.

Ad Formats

Below, we provide a quick overview of ad formats and destinations.

Video

Tell your story with sight, sound and motion. Video ads come in a range of lengths and styles—from short, feed-based ads you watch on the go, to longer videos you watch on the couch.

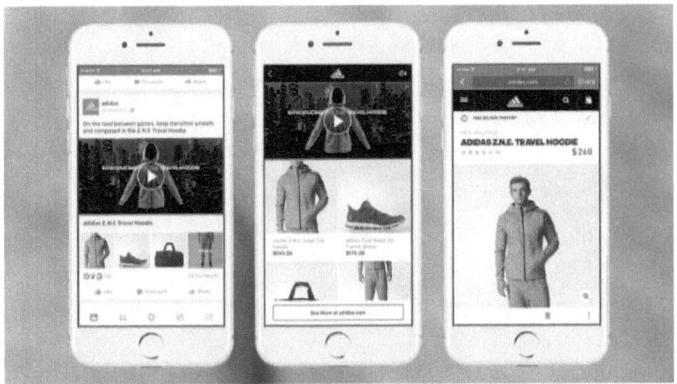

Photo

Photo ads offer a clean, simple format to feature engaging imagery and copy. Convey who you are and what you do through high-quality images or illustrations.

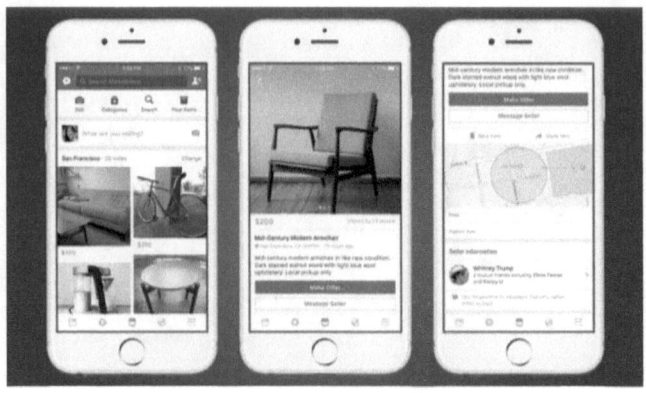

Stories

Stories are a customizable, edge-to-edge experience that lets you immerse people in your content. Tap into their passions and inspire them to take action on mobile.

 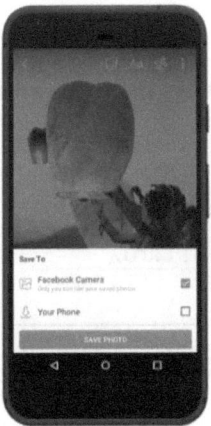 

Messenger

Messenger ads help people start conversations with your business. Get personal with current or potential customers and add interactive or automated features.

Carousel

Carousel ads let you showcase up to ten images or videos in a single ad, each with its own link. Highlight different products or tell a brand story that develops across each card.

Slideshow

Slideshow ads are video-like ads made of motion, sound and text. These lightweight clips help you tell your story beautifully across devices and connection speeds.

Collection

Collection ads let people discover, browse and buy what you offer. People can tap an ad to learn more about a specific product, all within a fast-loading experience.

Payables

Playable ads offer people an interactive preview before they download an app. Find higher intent users for your app with this try-before-you-buy experience.

 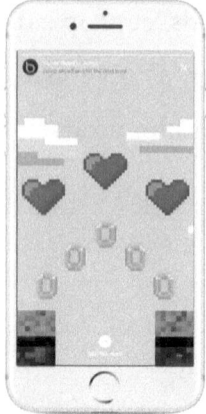 

Twitter

With 330 million monthly active users and various small business ad options, Twitter is a great platform for you to launch robust campaigns and to attract a wide array of potential customers.

Website clicks

Website clicks or conversions campaigns are optimized to drive traffic and generate conversions on your website from Tweets targeted to specific audiences. These campaigns allow you to feature your website content with Website Cards — a powerful ad format that allows users to preview an image, related context, and a clear call-to-action in their timeline.

Followers campaign

Followers campaigns allow you to promote your account and grow your audience on Twitter. Follower campaigns are displayed in multiple locations across the Twitter platform — including

Home Timelines, Who to Follow, and search results — and this suggestion is labeled as Promoted to distinguish it from other recommended accounts.

App installs

With app installs or re-engagements campaigns, you can drive users to download or open mobile apps directly from within a Tweet using App Cards — a powerful ad format that allows mobile users to preview an image, view app ratings, and install or open an app directly from their timelines. Twitter mobile app promotion campaigns are built to work on a cost per app click pricing system. This ensures you only pay for clicks that lead to the App Store or Google Play, or to open the app.

Tweet engagements campaign

Tweet engagements campaigns allow you to extend the reach of your content to a relevant audience on Twitter. You can promote Tweets that are published organically or choose to create Tweets that are only promoted to the audiences you target. You only pay when people you target engage with your content. Impressions that don't generate an engagement are free.

Awareness campaign

Awareness campaigns will help you reach more of your customers and drive better awareness for your brand. You set a bid amount per 1000 impressions (CPM) and the campaign will optimize for unique reach, which should deliver more reach for your campaigns at the same budget, with the same targeting and creative.

PARTY IN THE BACK, BUSINESS IN THE FRONT

To me, "Sales and Marketing" is the backbone of every successful business. I personally love the "Sales" part. I love the instant return on investment realized when you take your products directly to the consumer, or end user. But That's just me. Marketing is the one activity or set of activities that can be directly tied to your revenue and subsequently your profits.

Large corporations do not play games when it comes to attracting new customers. The average fortune 500 company spends 11 percent of their overall budgets on sales and marketing per year. Consumer packaged goods companies spend the most on marketing, coming in at around a quarter of their budgets per year.

The U.S. Small Business Administration recommends spending 7 to 8 percent of your gross revenue for marketing and advertising if you're doing less than $5 million a year in sales and your net profit margin. And although each company employs various forms of marketing, all running simultaneously, each is exploited with the precision and seriousness required to produce a return on investment. Since you are reading this book, I assume you intend to make social media marketing one of, if not the main means by which you hope to attract new customers. If this is the case, then I urge that you take your social media marketing efforts seriously.

Start by separating your personal and business footprints. Each social media platform provides the tools needed to build a corporate image. Facebook allows you to build company pages, for example. Via these pages, you can deploy professional and stackable marketing campaigns.

TELL IT, DOENT SELL IT

Think of your social media campaign as one big story with your various ads being complete chapters of this story. Your overall story, of course, should be about your brand. What do you do? How do you do it? What do you stand for? etc. Your brand narrative should be lofty, and inspirational.

Your individual ads, however, should speak directly to your intended audience in a way that they can relate to. For example, eBay is a shopping destination, however, the company highlights its features based on whether they are, at any given time addressing a seller or buyer.

That being said, you should craft your ads in a way that does not simply ask the audience to buy something but to come on a journey with you. Your ads should be the "Once Upon a Time" part of your story, asking the prospect to stop whatever they are doing to hear you out. We will go deeper into this concept later when I lay out what makes an effective social media ad.

CHAPTER FIVE

SOCIAL MEDIA TIPS AND GUIDES: INSTAGRAM: BUILD YOUR INSTAGRAM FOLLOWING

TAKING THE ROAD LESS TRAVELED

There are various, "not so honest" methods out there that one can use to grow their Instagram following. You could buy followers, Although I would strongly advise against that. You could also employ the use of bots, and again, I would not recommend doing so either.

After all, your ultimate goal as a business owner is to grow a large-enough following of real users who are interested in your products and services.

That being said, with some patience, hard work and imagination, you can grow your Instagram following without having to resort to any shady methods.

We have discussed in previous chapters, the dominance of Instagram among younger audiences, and the need for you to create marketing campaigns to reach out to some of these folks. Below are a few tips to help you do just that.

Use relevant trending hashtags

Hashtags are like little roadmaps to help folks who are searching for topics, related to what you do, find your stuff. Using the relevant hashtags will ensure that the content you put out is discovered by people who are interested in your brand messaging and who are more likely to follow you on Instagram.

Tag your location

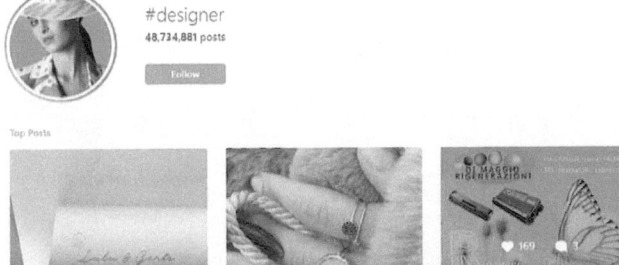

Here is a great way to get discovered by as many people on Instagram as possible. I would advise that you add a location tag whenever elements of your posts are location-based. Tag the location of your business (if applicable) and ask that your followers do the same.

Follow other notable users

In life, you get when you give. The same goes for Instagram and the whole social media experience. A sure bankable way to grow your Instagram following is by following others. Here you want to follow folks in your industry or at the very least, folks whose content is in some way relevant to yours. Follow only those with massive amounts of content and followers. They will follow you back and thus exposing your content to their followers as well.

Be Consistent

I don't need to tell you that consistency as one of the most overlooked pillars of success. Half of life is showing up, and I would add that you must show up and show up often. Success in social media marketing and building your Instagram following is no different.

Once you decide to try to build your following by posting engaging content, it is imperative to share fresh content on a predictably consistent basis. Doing so will help keep your audience engaged while you find new ones.

Post Engaging Content

To piggyback on the previous point, sharing relevant, engaging content will go a long way to grow your Instagram following. Yes, posting consistently is super important but so is posting engaging content. There are rules to this, one of the most important ones is to post visually pleasing content.

CHAPTER SIX

ANATOMY OF AN EFFECTIVE SOCIAL MEDIA AD + EXAMPLES

WHAT TO EXPECT

I am glad to see you make it this far. Thanks for your unwavering commitment to social media marketing. In this chapter, I will provide some details on a few topics I touched on previously. I will also explain why certain social ads are so effective while others fail to hit their targets. I will also walk you through the process of creating your very own killer ads and the essential elements needed to make your ads come alive.

OVERALL STRATEGY

Although there are some subtle differences in advertising across the top five social platforms, the basic strategy is pretty much the same. Most of the tips and information I share here in this book apply to Facebook, Twitter, Instagram, Linkedin, etc. I will let you know up front when I am providing platform-specific information. These, I will try to separate into different chapters to avoid any confusion.

My goal here is to provide you with an overall strategy and specific details, when I can, to help you create and launch successful social media marketing campaigns, regardless of which specific platforms you ultimately choose to work with. I deliberately focus a lot on paid campaigns, although I will provide some tips and strategies for developing your firm's brand on social media via unpaid means.

I focus on the *Paid* side of things for two reasons: 1. This is the arena in which I have the most experience, and 2. I stand by my belief that one can only truly build a strong marketing infrastructure via paid means. But That's just my opinion.

LET'S RECAP

To understand the most effective ways Social

media can be used as a marketing tool for your business, we must first consider a couple of things. The first of which is, that most folks on Social media are typically not actively looking to make a purchase or spend their hard-earned money on anything on the site. They are there to connect with friends but will try out something interesting and/or free.

We must also understand the difference between annoying your friends by posting content on your personal social media pages and actually paying to advertise your product on Social media.

There are a bunch of folks who have struggled to successfully promote their products or services using Social media. Most organic campaigns fail to deliver the desired results for a Plethora of reasons.

ELEMENTS OF AN EFFECTIVE SOCIAL MEDIA AD

As I have stated before in previous chapters, Social ads are different from most types of digital, and even analog ads. Social ads are unique in the sense that while most ads seek to provide actionable intel on products already being previewed or searched for by their target audience, Social advertising by its very nature is meant to be disruptive.

These are ads that are meant to stop you in your proverbial tracks and ask, no demand that you pay attention. This is the reason why most successful ads are vividly visual, straight-to-the-point and will typically use emotional language. You see this phenomenon clearly when it comes to political ads when the producer of the ad uses sounds, visuals, and language meant to stir up emotions. For better or worse, these ads are very effective in the social media universe.

That being said, before we tackle the technical elements of effective social ads, let's take a bird's eye view of the things that you should keep in mind when building your ads.

Start here

Visual

Social media is a very "Visual' medium. That's just what it is. There really is no way to get around that fact. You can have the most compelling product/offer, but if you fail to capture the aesthetic senses of others, your brand will fail to garner the attention you need.

I remember when I first read about the concept behind Instagram, back then when the site had just launched. I thought, "this will never work". I mean who would spend their time just checking out and commenting on other people's pictures?" Turns out, a lot of people actually.

I consider this the first rule of social media marketing, or any kind of marketing campaign for that matter. Be sure to use captivating, quality, high-resolution photos and videos for your social ads.

Video is always better

Basically, anytime you have the opportunity to use video content within your ads, take it. All available data shows that video is far more engaging than any other kind of content online. According to HubSpot, 90% of users say that product videos are helpful in the decision process. SmallBizTrends reports that Social video generates 12 times the shares than text and images combined. Video posts on Facebook have 135% greater organic reach than photo posts, according to Social Media Today, and After watching a video, 64% of users are more likely to buy a product online (Source: HubSpot).

Examples

Elements of effective social ads: Video is always better (Examples)

Direct

Save the flowery inspirational language for your 30 or 60-second television spot. That kind of lingo is best reserved for your company brochures and website.

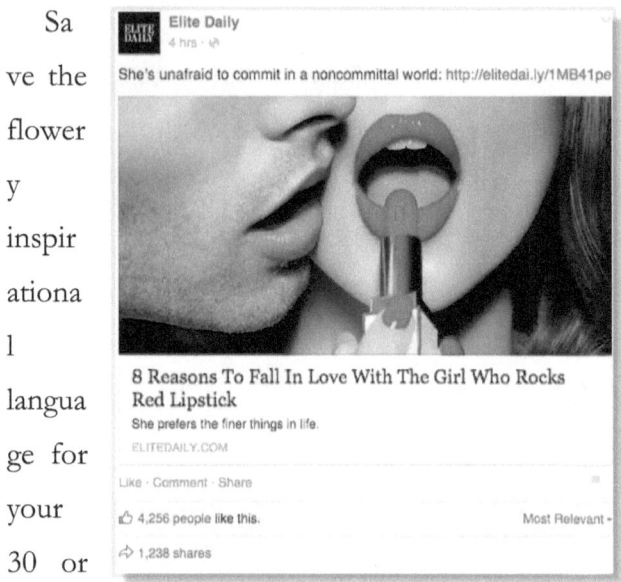

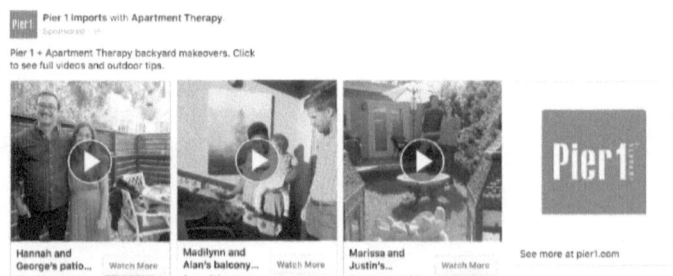

When it comes to social media marketing, your ad copy should be as direct, brief, and relatable as possible.

Since your ads will be constructed to appeal to a specific kind of person with a specific profession and specific interests, you want to "speak their language". You can even feel free to use industry jargon if you want to. Sure, no one else will fully understand the ad other than those in the industry, but guess what? You don't want anyone else.

Emotional

The thing about people and emotions is not so

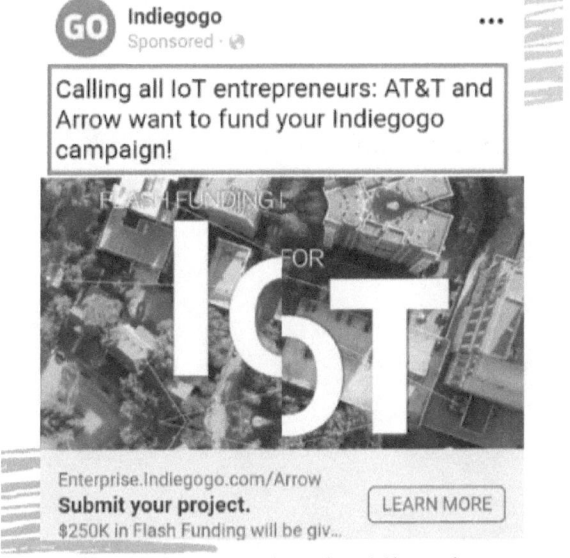

much, as some are emotional while others are not,

nope. It's that some respond to a wider array of emotional stimuli than others. It's more of a range and which kinds of emotions motivate us. My point is, we are all, in one way or another, emotional.

Ever watch a daytime TV commercial for Life insurance? You will notice an emphasis on such fears as not being able to get coverage due to health issues,

or the idea of not being able to afford coverage, or rather the guarantee that cost of coverage will not increase with age. So, let's recap; depleting health and cost increase. These ads target seniors. These will be foreign concepts to one who is young and healthy, and not on a fixed income. Social media ads tend to be heavy on emotional motivators. Find out which your target audience responds to and use them in your ads.

Example

Elements of effective social ads: Emotional (Example)

Convenient

This particular rule applies to any product or service delivery strategy. I started out selling life insurance, and despite the fact that there are literally thousands of insurance agents, agencies and consultants in my city, my wife and I were able to build our business simply because we were willing to visit folks where they lived and worked, and help them get coverage.

While other agents sat waiting for folks to come to their offices, we went directly to our customers. Sometimes, driving hours and hours just to sit with folks at their kitchen tables to talk about insurance. The key to our success? We made it convenient for folks to access the service we were offering. Everybody loves convenience.

It's the reason most McDonald's restaurants on any given day will see more people come through the Drive-thru than use their lobby to place orders. Use this principle with your social media marketing as well. Make it quick and easy for your intended target to take the action you need them to take. I can't tell you how many times I see ads that ask you to "learn more" only to require that you fill out a long form, then check your email in order to receive the promised info.

Don't be that person. If it's contact info you seek, ask for what is the most important, yet easy-to-give, like their email for example, and once you have the prospect in your contact list, proceed to strategically ask for the rest of the info as time goes on.

CREATING YOUR SOCIAL MEDIA AD

Any Social Media Ad will have certain basic elements. This is true across Facebook, Twitter, Instagram, and Linkedin. These are the parts that when added up, form your whole ad. Each part needs to be strategically constructed with specific language in order for your ad to pack the punch that you need. In this section, I will discuss the elements of a successful social media ad based on my own personal experience. I will provide you with some tips to help boost each element in order for you to find success in your marketing efforts.

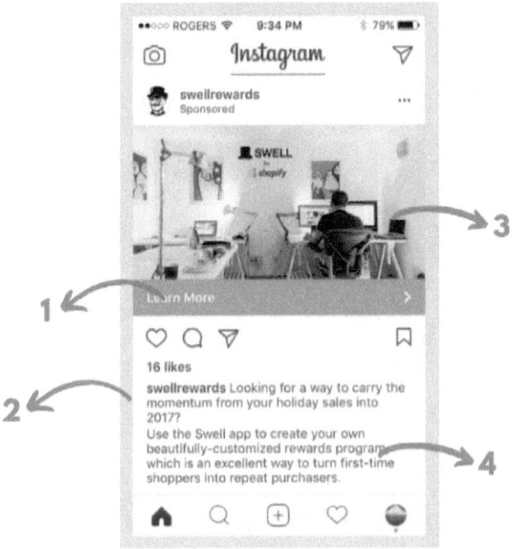

1. Create a clear call to action

Every Social media ad fall into one of two categories: ads built to grab your prospect's attention and ads designed to drive a direct action such as sales, app install, or to generate leads. You want to build your ad with absolute clarity on which of these you wish to accomplish. An ad that tries to create brand awareness and initiate a transaction will most certainly fail. You want to decide on one simple action you want people to take. With that in mind, you will want to decide which type Call to action does the job for you.

Examples of direct-action CTA's

- Request a demo
- Shop now
- Start a free trial

Examples of brand awareness CTA's

- Follow our page
- Learn more
- Get your free copy today
- Like our page

2. Write a clear tone-appropriate headline

Your ideal Social media ad headline should not be overly wordy, listing a bunch of random features and benefits. Use a conversational tone and speak directly to the needs and wants of your intended audience.

When it comes to ad headlines, there really is no set playbook to follow. I would recommend checking out ads by bigger brands in your industry to see how they do it, then try a few out to see which ones get the best results. Then, build upon the ones that get the most responses and eliminate the ones that don't cut it. Do this until you master the text and tonality needed to accomplish your desired goals.

3. Use high quality relevant images / videos

As I have stated before, the images or videos you use in your ad is one of the most important elements of any social media campaign. Choose your photos and/or videos carefully. Be sure to use high-resolution images or videos that are sure to grab the attention of your audience but also tell a story. Your audience should have some idea as to what your ad is about by just looking at your photo or the screenshot of your video. At the very least, they should be intrigued enough to stop and check it out.

4. Description

Your Ad's description is your opportunity to entice your prospect to take the action you require. Here, you still want to be direct, but a bit more descriptive. Keep in mind that you can create many different kinds of ads for a single campaign, so don't try to pack everything into this section. Highlight a few features and benefits specifically relevant to your audience. Also let them know what to expect once they take action.

CHAPTER SEVEN

THESE GUYS GET IT: COMPANIES THAT HAVE USED SOCIAL MEDIA EFFECTIVELY

In the previous chapter, we looked at both strategic and technical elements of any effective social media ad. I strongly believe that you are best served if you first ask yourself what your overall ad theme(s) will be. Then, carefully craft each of the technical aspects of your ads with your desired end results in mind.

To give you some inspiration, in this chapter I will highlight a few of the wildly popular social media campaigns we have seen recently, from well-known brands. I will give you my opinion on what I think makes these ads effective and how you can incorporate some of the elements used to boost your social media marketing efforts.

User-Generated Content

User-generated social media campaigns are great for showing a brands connection to its audience and the brand's goodwill with users and fans. This type of ad is all about sharing content that your customers have created. These types of campaigns are very popular among Fashion and Lifestyle brands. Below are a few brands that have employed this strategy beautifully to create brand awareness and to generate sales.

Cupshe

www.cupshe.com

Cupshe is a swimsuit brand that focuses almost exclusively on user-generated content in their Instagram strategy.

Pro tip

The company lets its followers know exactly what to do to be featured. They also proudly display comments made by their users to show that they are favored by their customers. You can use both strategies to help build a cult following for your brand.

cupshe ✓ Following

1,451 posts   796k followers   16 following

Cupshe
☀ Affordable chic swimwear made for living your best life under the sun
🏖 Tag @cupshe to be featured
🇩🇪 @cupshe_de
🇫🇷 @cupshe_fr
🇪🇸 @cupshe_es
👉 Shop now 👈
have2have.it/cupshe

Lush Cosmetics

www.lushusa.com

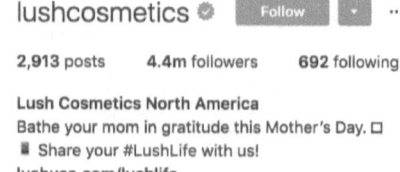

Lush Cosmetics is another brand that uses a hashtag for its user-generated content campaigns. Within Lush Cosmetics' Instagram bio, they ask followers to "Share your #LushLife with us!" This encourages fans to submit their own content directly to Lush through the #LushLife Instagram hashtag.

For the brand, when users include #LushLife as a hashtag on their posts, the brand is able to see a collection of all user-generated content in one place.

Cross-Channel Promotion

With this particular strategy, you will use various different social media platforms to try to reach your audience. Below is an example of a company that employs this type of strategy very effectively.

Casper

www.casper.com

Casper, the mattress company does this very well. They also have a strong presence on other, not-so-popular platforms like IGTV, Spotify, and YouTube. On these Video Channels they promote their Sleep Channel. The company shares each new Sleep Channel episode on all three video/music platforms (Spotify, YouTube & IGTV) while also promoting a teaser on their other social media profiles. This is the perfect way to generate buzz around their sleep channel, increase their following on other platforms and cross-promote content.

Pro tip

Think of ways in which you can stand out among your competitors with your social media marketing strategy. Feel free to be different, finding ways to use platforms that may not seem so obvious.

Humor

Using humor is always a great way to grab people's attention and make a lasting impression. Many well-known brands use this strategy to attract a large following on social media.

MoonPie

www.moonpie.com

MoonPie is a vintage snack brand which posts a lot of quirky insights on social media. The company started getting a lot of attention after it launched Twitter beef with Hostess Snacks over whose treat was the official snack of the solar eclipse in the summer of 2017.

Pro tip

Do not be afraid to create a bit of friction with other brands to boost your social media profile and get your ads seen by a lot more people. You can do all this in good, clean fun of course, challenging some of your competitors or sharing your "brand's opinions" about current events.

Denny's

www.dennys.com

Denny's got in on a popular Twitter meme that tricks the viewer into repeatedly zooming in on spots on a picture to read secret messages. But Denny's also tweets clever remarks commenting on hot topics circulating -- like the running joke of 2017, when social media accounts kept creating different ways to copy Snapchat Stories.

CONCLUSION

These are just a few examples of very effective social media campaigns and promotional strategies we have seen other brands use recently. It is important to pick which image you wish your brand to be associated with and stick with it.

If you choose humor as your thing, then you

want to remain consistent with this theme as much as you can. I hope you, at this point, are able to start to conceptualize where you think your brand fits into the social media universe, and how you plan to employ both free and paid social media tools to help promote your products and services.

CHAPTER EIGHT

SOCIAL MEDIA TIPS AND GUIDES: GET MORE VIEWS ON YOUTUBE

SECOND MOST VISITED SITE

As an entrepreneur, you simply cannot afford to miss out on this great opportunity to get the word out about your product or services to YouTube's large community of users. With over 1.9 billion daily active users, YouTube, believe it or not, is the second most visited site on the Internet. Second only to Google.com. 50 million of those users are content creators who upload 576,000 hours of video to YouTube every day.

Folks love YouTube for the same reason as they enjoy spending time on platforms like Instagram and Pinterest. For the most part, these apps do not require much effort to consume data and are highly visual. People across the globe spend millions of hours each year on YouTube, watching all kinds of videos, from makeup tutorials to long-form documentaries about " The secrets of the solar system".

On YouTube, you will have a chance to create

free content for your desired audiences and also deploy paid marketing content. Regardless of which strategy you choose, the most important thing is to get your videos/content seen by as many people in your target audience as possible.

Just like with other Social platforms, YouTube gives you the ability to choose which folks you want to see your ads. The platform does not provide the specificity of targeting associated with Facebook, but there are some things you can do to make your content more accessible to the folks you are trying to reach.

Use descriptive, Keyword-rich video titles

Choose precise descriptive titles for your videos with popular keywords. Use terms like "how-to," "why does," etc.

When you blog about your videos, make the blog titles the same as the video titles, and make sure the title tag of your page matches the title of the blog post and videos.

When ranking videos, Google primarily considers the match between search keywords and the video title. Google likes it when the title tag of the page matches the title of the video and will give a higher weighting for results where this is the case.

Write dynamic video descriptions

Don't just put a few words in the description of the video. Tell a story using your keywords. Add your whole site URL at the very top of the description, including the http://. This puts a link back to your site in the description. This will allow YouTube to transcribe your content.

Use Eye-catching thumbnail images

Most folks online do not read. They instead rely on the visual aspects of the content they scan to make decisions. By carefully picking a thumbnail for your video that is both visual and intriguing, you will be able to attract twice as many people to see your content. Ninety percent of the top-performing videos on YouTube use dynamic, thought-provoking images as their thumbnails. YouTube even encourages its users to use custom thumbnails and recommends that you consider which thumbnail you will use even before you start shooting your video.

Your custom thumbnail should be 1280 x 720 pixels and less than 2 MB in size, in JPG, .GIF, .BMP, or .PNG format.

Keep it short.

Shorter 1-2-minute videos perform better than longer videos on YouTube. Hook viewer in first 10 seconds – Expect to lose 20% of your audience within first 10 seconds of playback. Check your YouTube Insight Hot Spots to find where you're losing people. Practice packing your entire message, or at least a bulk of it into the first 30 seconds of your videos. Try to do this even with your free content. Most folks will drift off after about a minute into any videos and instead start focusing on other potential videos they could watch.

Use playlists to hold people's attention

According to YouTube, top-performing brands promote 2x as many playlists as the bottom 25%. Big brands have spent lots of money on research, and they know and understand the power of auto-play. It is very difficult to stop watching videos if more videos that you might like simply start to play automatically. One after the other. Most folks will keep watching as long as you produce great, compelling content.

CHAPTER NINE

SOCIAL MEDIA TIPS AND GUIDES: USE LINKEDIN NATIVE VIDEO TO REACH NEW AUDIENCES

GONE ARE THE DAYS

When LinkedIn was viewed as merely a boring B2B social media platform. A place to go to build serious professional relationships. In a continued effort to appeal to a wider audience and improve user experience, Linkedin launched native video in 2017. This new feature allows users to upload videos to share. Currently, the feature is only available on the Linkedin mobile app.

Linkedin native videos generated over 300 million impressions over a twelve-month period. According to the Microsoft-owned social networking site, native videos are five times more likely to spark conversation among users than other forms of content.

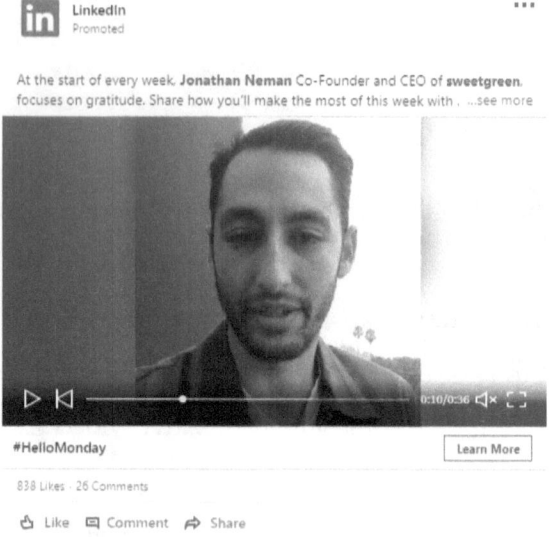

What is Linkedin native video?

Native video is a robust, feature-rich tool designed to allow Linkedin users to share content in the most digestible way available today: Video. Video is the most consumed kind of content online and via mobile.

Linkedin video aims to allow users to upload professional videos to share with other users. The most popular types of videos on the platform are videos of members *giving career advice, words of inspiration, and how-to, entrepreneurial-type videos.*

This is an opportunity for you to create content to share on Linkedin, especially if you offer services and products to other businesses. Native Videos will provide you with a great way to reach out to other professionals and entrepreneurs in a cost-effective way. Not to mention, by doing so, you will be reaching out to the type of audience there on the platform ready and willing to connect with other professionals. These types of folks are always open to hear about new products and services. LinkedIn users typically use the platform to find relevant content, meaning they'll be much more willing to check out what you're sharing.

Get this; according to the company, out of Linkedin's 500 million plus users, 61 million are senior level influencers and 40 million are in decision-making positions. LinkedIn is the most-used social media platform amongst Fortune 500 companies.

According to LinkedIn's Sophisticated

Marketer's Guide to LinkedIn, 94% of B2B marketers use LinkedIn as a content distribution channel, compared to Twitter at 89%, Facebook and YouTube both at 77%, and Google+ 61%. If you have content to distribute (which you definitely should), LinkedIn should be your first stop. It's where most B2B marketers go first.

Your video posted on July 18, 2017 (51 comments, 257 likes)
18,139 views

772 people who have the title Salesperson viewed your video		Your biggest audience is from Greater New York City Area	
CEO / Executive Director	450	San Francisco Bay Area	242
Business / Corporate Strategist	241	Greater Chicago Area	234
Marketing Specialist	181	Greater Atlanta Area	135
Business Owner	176	Greater Philadelphia Area	135

Show more

Most of your views came from your 2nd+ degree network

How Entrepreneurs can benefit from native videos

Business owners and marketers can position themselves to benefit immensely by building a content sharing strategy around native videos. Videos are the best way to share your brand's story in this new fast-paced digital environment.

Videos are already popular and well-adapted by the general public. Get this, 45 percent of people watch more than an hour of Facebook or YouTube videos a week, more than 500 million hours of videos are watched on YouTube each day. More video content is uploaded in 30 days than the major U.S. television networks have created in 30 years, and 87% of online marketers use video content to get their brand messaging out to the public.

As an entrepreneur, you simply cannot afford to avoid video as part of your digital marketing plan(s).

With a highly focused content distribution strategy built around Linkedin native video, you, the entrepreneurs will have the opportunity to reach a targeted audience who will not be distracted by other types of trivial videos. These folks will be in professional mode and ready to absorb your content. Research from Cisco Systems found that 75% of business executives watch work-related video weekly.

How to Upload Native Video on LinkedIn

To share native video on LinkedIn, open the app on your mobile device. In the share box on the home screen, tap the video camera icon.

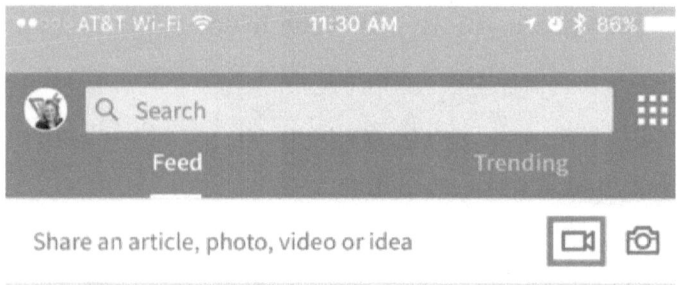

On the next screen, choose a pre-recorded video from your camera roll or click Video to record a video on the spot (your video will automatically be saved to your camera roll).

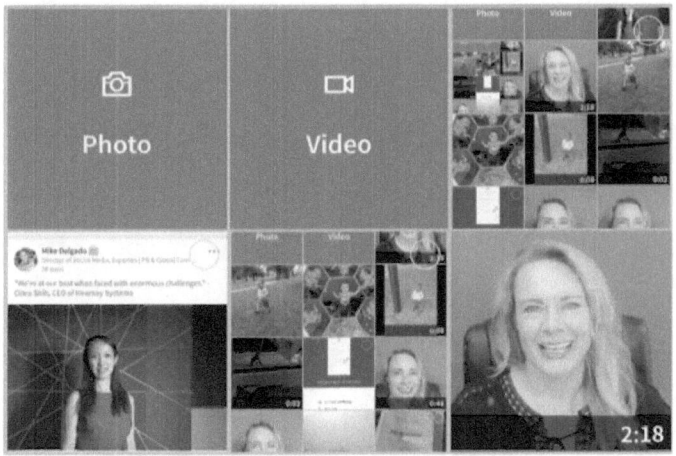

LinkedIn has some basic requirements for native video. The video must be at least 3 seconds long and can't exceed 10 minutes. The maximum file size is 5GB. Remember, people have short attention spans, so it's a good idea to keep your videos shorter than 3 minutes.

Add text (up to 700 characters) to your update to describe your video. (You can do this before or after you upload the video.) Be sure to include talking points to encourage people to watch. For example, outline the steps for a how-to video, or write a short update that teases the content and link to a longer blog or LinkedIn Publisher post.

Tip: If you don't want to compose the update text on your device, send yourself an email with the text or write the update on a cloud-based app such as Notes, Evernote, or Google Docs. Then copy and paste it into LinkedIn.

As with normal updates, add links, tag people if you mention them, and include relevant hashtags.

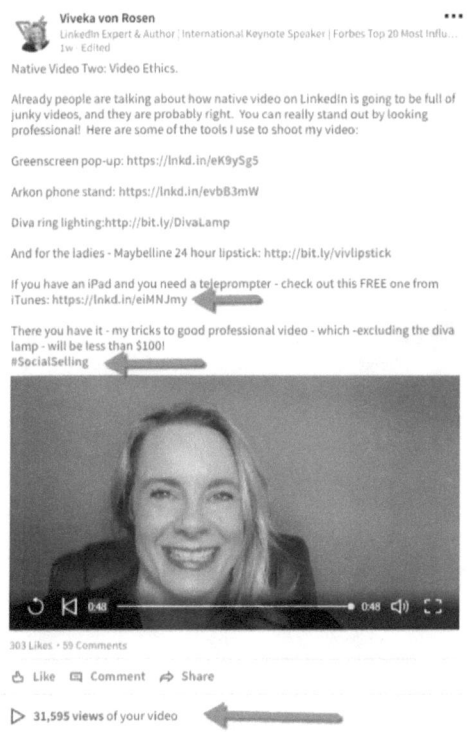

When you're finished, tap Post just as you would for a regular update. On an Android phone, you can do other things while your video is posting. However, on an iPhone, you need to stay in the app.

Note: Your native video will play automatically in the feed with the sound off. Viewers will have to unmute the audio to listen to it.

LinkedIn also lets you add the native video link to your profile via the mobile app. Click the three dots icon at the top right of your post and choose Copy Link to Post.

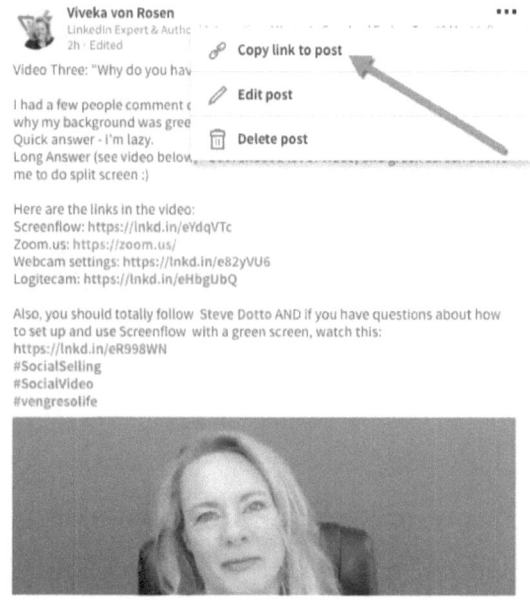

Then go into your profile settings, edit your intro section, and upload the video to Media. You can also add video link to any Media section or share the link on Facebook.

Want to add video to Publisher? Take a screenshot of the video, copy the video link, and then link the image to the video.

Video Marketing Engagement by the numbers.

- 51% of marketing professionals worldwide name video as the type of content with the best ROI.

- Marketers who use video grow revenue 49% faster than non-video users.

- Sixty-four percent of consumers make a purchase after watching branded social videos (via tubularinsights).

- 59% of executives agree that if both text and video are available on the same topic, they are more likely to choose video.

- Social video generates 1200% more shares

than text and images combined.

- Views on branded video content have increased 258% on Facebook and 99% on YouTube as of June 2017 (via tubularinsights).

CHAPTER TEN

**SOCIAL MEDIA TIPS AND GUIDES:
HASHTAG YOUR WAY TO SUCCESS**

IF YOU EVER WONDERED WHAT HASHTAGS REALLY ARE

Simply put, Hashtags (#) are neat little phrases or words that will allow your content to be added into a stream of related posts on social media. Using the "right" hashtags will allow your otherwise unpopular posts to be seen by more people.

According to a Wikipedia definition, a Hashtag is a type of metadata tag used on social networks such as Twitter and other microblogging services, allowing users to apply dynamic, user-generated tagging which makes it possible for others to easily find messages with a specific theme or content.

More science than art

When looking to reach a maximum number of followers, you must carefully consider which Hashtags to use for your Tweets, Facebook posts, and your Instagram pictures. Picking the right Hashtags for your social media posts should be more science than art.

Choose popular Hashtags and watch your posts reach a considerable amount of people across multiple online platforms. On the other hand, choosing non-performing hashtag can cause your posts to reach virtually no one. There are various steps and points to consider when choosing the best Hashtags.

The Big Picture

One of the main reasons to use Hashtags with your social media posts is to reach people with posts based on topics they are already interested in. It is also important to consider Hashtags that are not saturated or overused. Using saturated hashtags will do nothing to get your posts seen. Your content, in this case, will just be added to the other millions of posts on the same topic and will not be easily discovered. Your stuff will just be added to a heap.

So, for example, let's imagine that you have a post about the movie Black Panther. The temptation here might be to use #blackpanthermovie. This seems logical because almost everyone saw the movie and it will get a lot of searches, right? The issue here is that your post will almost certainly be buried, with all the billions of posts about the movie and all.

One other way to go around this issue is to use hashtags from other popular aspects of the movie that are popular but not too popular. You can also use any of the various tools out there to assess which black panther related hashtags might work better for you.

How will I know which hashtags to use?

A few years ago, just when hashtags were becoming popular, you had to employ quite a bit of guesswork when trying to figure out which tags would get you the most views, likes, and shares. These days, there are tools like All#Hashtag (https://all-hashtag.com) and hashtagify (https://hashtagify.me) to help decide which of the many trending phrases will do the trick. I use both of these tools to boost my own social media posts. Both tools work quite the same. With both tools, you can simply look up a phrase or word relevant to

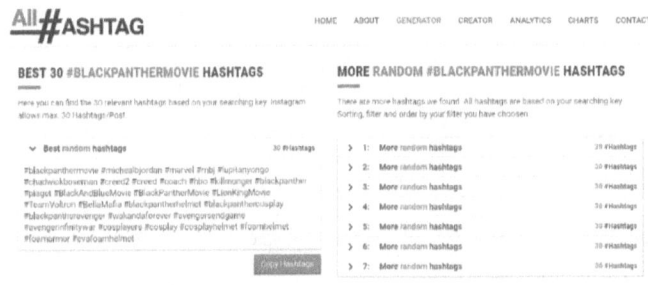

your post and get a detailed look at which other similar phrases are trending, and who else is out there talking about the same topic. Also, with either tool, you will also get a detailed analysis of each suggested hashtag.

Alternative Hashtag Strategies

When looking for these kinds of terms, you can also think about particular niches, as well as things that are currently in style or popular. For example, you should consider posting images and Tweets that respond to what's currently in the news and what's currently trending.

You can put out posts in which you review or provide your opinions about popular news items. If a big event happens, this will likely get a lot of searches and you can get in on that action before the market is saturated with related posts.

This strategy works best on YouTube, where users get thousands of views by putting out videos reviewing popular movies and songs.

Finally, consider using hashtags that relate to an event in your local news environment. These will be very popular but the total number of people posting those images will be limited geographically or by attendance. Just been to an Expo? Perfect opportunity for some related Tweets!

Are there benefits to using Hashtags?

Sure, there are! And we have covered a few in this chapter already. Some other great advantages of using hashtags are:

- **Grow your social media following-** Using hashtags, over time will help you build a large following. This goal can be boosted if you focus on an area of expertise. Over time folks will come to see you as an expert in that particular field and will decide to follow you.

- **Branding-** You can use Hashtags to help build brand awareness for your business. You can create branded Hashtags (e.g. #suzzies_dicount_mart), then use these in all your customer communications. Your customers will start to click on this hashtag to follow your updates on social media.

- **Competitive edge**- See what folks online are saying about your competitors. See where they fall short, and you can capitalize on.

- **Increase viewership** -You can grow viewership for your blog articles, videos, and other types of content by using hashtags. Since folks use keywords to search for stuff online, using hashtags will allow consumers to easily fins and consume your content.

- **Increase Revenue** - Grow your bottom line with Hashtags. Checking out what people are talking about online, across various social media platforms will guide your product development efforts. You will be able to easily tap into the needs of your audience and fill any gaps in the marketplace.

CHAPTER ELEVEN

SETTING OBJECTIVES AND MEASURING SUCCESS

THE END OF THE ROAD

I am glad to see you make it to the end of this book. Well, this is it; the final chapter. Now, I want to address just a couple of things. This will not take long at all. I want to talk about the part of social media marketing that most folks fail at. Heck, I think the lack of a plan and clear objectives and the patience to allow the plan to come together is the Achilles heel of most people in almost every endeavor in life.

We all, in some way lack the ability to carefully plan stuff out, and the patience to allow the plan to work. That being said, let's jump in.

What do you want?

This is a question I often ask myself before I build any social media campaign. I must know, or be able to start to define, to myself what I, in the long term and short term want out of my efforts.

Answering this question as succinctly as

possible helps me measure success, and also aids in the overall crafting of each ad in my campaign.

So, what do you want out of your campaign? Do you want to, in the short term educate your target audience on your new product? Do you want a percentage of folks who see your ads to take a specific action to get more info? Or do you want to initiate transactions with your ads? I think knowing what you want is an integral part of setting objectives.

Any budget will do

One of the great things about social marketing is that it's cheap. No joke. You only need a few bucks to get your message seen by folks across the world. There is no way to do that with radio or TV. Even large corporations don't spend as much money as you might think on social media ads.

Don't believe me? Use Facebook's Ad Library tool (https://www.facebook.com/ads/library/) to look up the ad spend of your largest competitor and you will see what I mean.

Sure, the ROI on social ads is lower than that of any other kind of direct marketing effort but social and it's lower barrier to entry allows companies of all sizes to experiment with various campaign ideas and to inexpensively figure out which ads are viable and which ones need to be retired.

Facebook Ad Library

Would you know success if it bit you on your ads?

My first rule when it comes to social media marketing, even before I create a plan is to define "success", and I always measure success as a factor of whether or not the end result justifies the initial investment.

I use the word " justify " simply because not all efforts in marketing and business for the matter will produce a monetary return. Some investments in your community, for example, are meant to build goodwill and show that there are actual people running the business, not just profit-hungry Androids. With that in mind, I want you to examine each marketing campaign and be honest with yourself as to what a " win" will look like, and what your next move is once you hit that goal. Sure, there are other factors that will go into making this determination but knowing success when you see it is a good place to start.

THANK YOU!

Hey there, good to see you made it to the end of this book. I hope you were able to extract some value here. I hope the information I have provided will effectively aid you in your social media marketing efforts.

I hope you can take the information provided here and build a remarkable social media marketing system, one that will help you grow your business as well as your brand.

Thank you.

NOTES

https://en.wikipedia.org/wiki/Timeline_of_social_media

https://www.forbes.com/sites/forbesnonprofitcouncil/2017/06/19/tapping-into-the-power-of-social-media/#7f74fe95ac00

https://sproutsocial.com/insights/topics/social-media-for-small-business/

https://blog.hootsuite.com/twitter-demographics/

https://blog.hootsuite.com/youtube-stats-marketers/

https://sproutsocial.com/insights/facebook-stats-for-marketers/

https://sproutsocial.com/insights/facebook-stats-for-marketers/

https://blog.hootsuite.com/instagram-statistics/

https://business.instagram.com/advertising/

https://business.twitter.com/en/solutions/twitter-ads.html

https://business.twitter.com/en/solutions/twitter-ads.html?ref=en-btc-solutions-footer

https://www.walletally.com/main/benefits-of-social-media-marketing-for-small-businesses

https://www.walletally.com/main/how-can-social-media-help-a-business-grow-3-tips-to-help-manage-your-business-accounts

https://business.twitter.com/en/solutions/twitter-ads.html?ref=en-btc-solutions-footer

https://www.walletally.com/main/5-easy-ways-to-get-free-instagram-followers-instantly

https://www.walletally.com/main/the-3-essential-elements-of-a-successful-facebook-marketing-campaign

https://blog.hootsuite.com/perfect-ad-facebook-minutes/

https://sproutsocial.com/insights/social-media-marketing-examples/

https://blog.hubspot.com/marketing/sassiest-social-media-brands

https://www.walletally.com/main/how-to-get-more-views-on-youtube-3-effective-tactics

https://blog.hootsuite.com/get-views-youtube/

https://www.walletally.com/main/why-facebook-advertising-is-effective-for-reaching-a-global-audience

https://www.socialmediaexaminer.com/linkedin-native-video-how-to-use/

https://www.walletally.com/main/why-you-should-be-using-linkedin-video-in-2019

https://foundationinc.co/lab/b2b-marketing-linkedin-stats/

https://www.walletally.com/main/how-to-use-hashtags-in-social-media-marketing

https://blog.dlvrit.com/hashtag/

https://all-hashtag.com/index.php
https://hashtagify.me

ABOUT THE AUTHOR

Frank is the Co-Founder of Corves Web Services: A software services firm located in Charlotte, NC. He loves starting new companies and bringing new products and services to market. He also loves to write in his spare time, focusing mostly on topics with which he can speak with some authority. He has published several books on sales, entrepreneurship, and marketing. He is an avid reader and a lover of the arts and sciences. Mostly astronomy and marine biology.

OTHER BOOKS BY FRANK:

- Recurring Revenue: A Practical Guide to help you launch your very own Software-as-a-service business

- Email Marketing in A Digital Age: Learn how to attract new customers through the power of Email Marketing and Social Media

- PERSONA: A proven step-by-step guide to identifying and attracting profitable customers to your new business

READING LIST

I recommend checking out these books that I have found to be helpful in trying to figure out how to best use social media to grow your business.

- The 1-Page Marketing Plan: Get New Customers, Make More Money, And Stand Out from The Crowd
  by Allan Dib

- One Million Followers: How I Built a Massive Social Following in 30 Days
  by Brendan Kane

- Influencer: Building Your Personal Brand in the Age of Social Media
  by Brittany Hennessy

- VENTURE! A Simple guide to help you

survive your first year in business

by Gathoni Njenga

The
Social Media HandBook

Harness the power of Social media to grow your small business

FRANK DAPPAH

OSTRICH™
Ostrich Publishers
Made in the U.S.A
www.ostrichpress.com

www.ingramcontent.com/pod-product-compliance
Lightning Source LLC
Chambersburg PA
CBHW021818170526
45157CB00007B/2632